THE POETRY GAMES

NORFOLK

Edited By Elle Berry

First published in Great Britain in 2018 by:

Young Writers
Remus House
Coltsfoot Drive
Peterborough
PE2 9BF
Telephone: 01733 890066
Website: www.youngwriters.co.uk

Book Design by Ashley Janson

SB ISBN 978-1-78896-596-5
Printed and bound in the UK by BookPrintingUK
Website: www.bookprintinguk.com
YB0364L

FOREWORD

Since 1991 our aim here at Young Writers has been to encourage creativity in children and to inspire a love of the written word. Each competition is tailored to the relevant age group, hopefully giving each student the inspiration and incentive to create their own piece of creative writing, whether it's a poem or a short story. We truly believe that seeing their work in print gives students a sense of achievement and pride.

For our latest competition The Poetry Games, secondary school students were given the challenge to stand up for what they believe in using nothing but the power of the pen. Using poetry as their tool, these aspiring poets were given the opportunity to express their thoughts and feelings on the topics that matter to them through verse.

Whilst skilfully conveying their opinions through poetry, the writers showcased in this collection have simultaneously managed to give poetry a breath of fresh air, brought it to life and made it relevant to them. Using a variety of themes and styles, these featured poets leave a lasting impression of their inner thoughts and feelings, making this anthology a rare insight into the next generation.

CONTENTS

THE POEMS

ANGER

I'm usually happy but there's one thing I get easily.
That's angry.
When I feel anger I feel fire in my head.
All rage burns inside me and I go red.
It's not a good feeling, I promise you that.
It always makes me want to smash something with a bat.
There's many things that make me rage like video games, bullies and more.
Sometimes I go upstairs and slam my bedroom door.
But my anger is not as bad as my cousin Jim,
Once you make him mad he goes ape crazy.
Calming me down is not easy.
All I need is to punch or kick something
And I feel better and calm.
But trust me, punching is not the right option for some.
Some of you breathe and you're better.
But not me - that never works.
Everyone is different wouldn't you agree?
There are some times when we get mad.
We can't stop it.
It's a daily thing in life.
If there's one thing you should learn from this poem -
Try to chill and don't let rage
Ruin you.

T-Jay Westall (14)
Broadland High School, Hoveton

WHAT HAPPENS WHEN I GET ANGRY

What happens when I get angry?
My cheeks go red
I burn up
I'm out of control
I'm scared
What am I going to do?
Who am I going to hurt?
I feel myself bubbling
Then I burn
My trust goes
What am I going to do?
Who am I going to hurt?
I only trust nature
But nature is against me
I want to run
What am I going to do?
I try to run
But I don't go anywhere
My legs go quicker
I still don't move
What am I going to do?
Everyone is against me
No one will help

My skin goes sensitive
I shiver
What am I going to do?
The plan changes
I break down
Then tears fall
I try to catch my breath
What am I going to do?
Who am I going to hurt?
I try to shout
No sound comes out
I try and try and try
Nothing works
What am I going to do?
Who am I going to hurt?

Hollie Buller (13)
Broadland High School, Hoveton

TING, TING, TING

Ting. Ting. Ting
Horrible messages from friends I'm not friends with anymore.
It makes me feel horrible inside
like I'm bubbling up, they don't have any feelings.
"You are a *very, very, very nasty girl*."
In full capital letters!
I was not very bothered anymore
even though it hurts inside.
I drove along the road and saw them.
The girls that tried to stop me.
But I was too busy and angry
I didn't stop.
I drove past them.
They got in their car
I could have really hurt them.
They followed me so I pulled over down a ditch
and they lost me.
I kept getting bad messages
so blocked them
and I didn't get any more horrible messages.
For a while.

Aaleyah Ramm (13)
Broadland High School, Hoveton

ANGER POEM

She keeps yelling
I can hear her from upstairs
I've done nothing wrong!

I'm starting to feel angry and annoyed
She's still shouting, screaming
My brain feels like it is going to explode like a volcano
I can't think what to say with all this stress
I wish she would stop before I break something
Or hit her by mistake
I really need to know what I have done
But she won't tell me.

All I feel like doing is breaking a window or a brick
I can't take this anger much longer
Before something bad happens to one of us.

So I just walk out slamming the front door. *Slam.*
Now I just need to find somewhere
For a while.

Keenan Wright (14)
Broadland High School, Hoveton

ANGER

I'm hot, I'm sweating.
The feeling inside me
is trying to rip my skin
and break free.
It feels like there is
A demonic demon inside
trying to break out.
I have goosebumps on
My back, legs and arms.
My skin goes sensitive.
I get tense.
It feels like there is
a force pushing against me.
I cannot move.
My head is throbbing.
My heart is beating.
I stop trying to move.
I relax and calm myself down.
I slowly lose the goosebumps.
My muscles start to relax.
My head stops throbbing.
I think,
Why didn't I do this before?

Kris Hayton (13)
Broadland High School, Hoveton

BOTTLED UP

I am angry
Shocked
Frightened of what I am going to do next
Shaking like a rattlesnake
Feel a burning sensation in my face.

Feel my fist clamp up like a vice
I can see my pulse pumping my blood around my body
My veins trying to rip out of my skin
My eyes looking around like a beady owl
I start to struggle to catch my breath
I can hear a voice whispering in my head
Feel like I am a fizzing bottle of coke
I feel like I am now about to pull the trigger

But suddenly it all stops...

Jannie O'Leary (14)
Broadland High School, Hoveton

ANGRY

When you are angry
you shake and wanna hurt someone,
or punch something.
And just give up.

You can't control yourself
and want to run away where nobody else is.
You can't think straight
It feels like you're burning inside.

You just want to scream and shout
And let it all out
Feel hot
And your hands begin to sweat.

You just need to explode
Like a car hitting a wall -
Bang!

Brad Thrower (13)
Broadland High School, Hoveton

ANGER

I was so angry I was shaking
I had a lump of sick in my stomach
I felt I was in a puddle of sweat
I wanted to scream, punch, cry, shout
My head felt like it would explode
Thoughts were going round and round again and again.
What am I going to do?
I try to scream, nothing comes out.
I try punch the wall but my hand doesn't reach it.
People against me, me against them.

Arabella Robertson (13)
Broadland High School, Hoveton

WHEN YOU ARE ANGRY

When you are angry,
A burning fire boils inside you,
It makes you shake,
Violently shake.

When you are angry,
It makes you mad,
Mental and monstrous,
Sometimes it makes you cry.

When you are angry
People smash things,
Violently smash things.

You erupt like a volcano
Bang!

Molly Mae London (14)
Broadland High School, Hoveton

UNTITLED

Anger makes you feel stressed.
Makes you shake and sweat.
Feel rage.
This is how anger makes me feel.
When you're angry
You sweat and shake.
I was
Raging.
Absolutely raging.
Being angry
Makes you throw things
and they smash.
Anger makes you
feel you want to explode
like a
Bomb!

Jake Pilgrim (13)
Broadland High School, Hoveton

POEM

People get angry
Upset when angry.
When angry you would
Want to smash things
You would want to
Take it out on other people
Just because you feel like it
And you have nothing else
To take it out on.
You would start to feel hot
And you want to lose control.

Kiraren Chrismas (14)
Broadland High School, Hoveton

YOU ARE NOT ALONE

The pain continues day after day
and you're seriously willing to stay?
When you're at home, you constantly feel alone.
You feel out of place, I can tell by the look on your face.
Your relationship is falling apart,
but he'll always be in your space.

She felt she was the one to blame for his actions
but she really wasn't making any sense.
All he did was put on an act and a face
hoping no one would see the demon in his trace.

He kicked, punched, screamed, spat
and all she thought was she could change and make her home a better place.
Refuse to let him hurt you
Take stand, speak up for yourself
and stay strong.
Dig deep inside for the inner strength to break away from the demon, the monster and the abuse
With everything it takes.

The road won't be easy but at least you will lead a life with dignity and freedom with what you will achieve.
Break free, you deserve so much more
As you won't be in that dreadful nightmare no more.

Danielle Louise Piggin (13)
Diss High School, Diss

EMPTY EXISTENCE

Looking out of the window
I see a cheery, red robin -
Perched on the branch of a blackberry bush.
Its belly looks fit to burst as it sings;
As it sings for the sheer joy of being alive.

Looking out of the window
I spy a bubbling, babbling brook -
Twisting and turning past the gnarled oak tree.
Ducks plummet to the ground and squat down;
Squat down to let the water gently suck at their webbed feet.

Looking out of the window
I observe delicate flowers unfurl -
Waking up and welcoming the beautifully bright day.
A dazzling array of petals are gently stretched out;
Stretched out so the whole world can admire them.

Looking back to my room
I glance a shimmering, black phone -
Daring me to step just a little bit nearer.
It's balancing precariously and just itching to be played.

Looking out of the window
I regretfully step backwards from the groping sun -
Hating all that I am leaving behind.

I feel my way half-heartedly to the buzzing device;
The buzzing device that glints evilly in the receding light.

I give a small sigh and slowly sink into my bed
Losing myself in the
All-enveloping
All-consuming
All-absorbing technology...

Bethany Ely (13)
Diss High School, Diss

THE SEA

As it sparkles under the moonlit sky,
Gently washing shells upon the golden sand,
The crashing upon the rocks,
Seeping its way through every little crack and gap,
Slowly weathering it away.

Gracefully swishing in the vast open space,
The sea ripples, gripples and pipples,
Not all of this tranquil place is calm,
Under the softest blue, like velvet waves,
Animals hunt in the most unlikely ways,
Ripping carcasses whole,
Gnawing on the flesh too stubborn to let go,
Racing each other to an easy meal,
It isn't all pretty.

I love this place for its differences,
From the sparkles of the moon,
To the unlit hole below,
Home to predators of all shapes and sizes,
Some may dislike it,
But I love it for this exact reason.

It's diverse
A lot like us.

Lex Dutton (12)
Diss High School, Diss

DO YOU REALISE?

Do you realise you're hurting me?
I just want you to leave me be,
It really hurts but you don't care,
Even though I say prayers upon prayers,
Do you realise what we could be?
Maybe friends, but you just don't see,
Our friendship is horrific and deadly,
And every day I have to be ready.
Do you realise the days of endless struggle?
You make my life like a never-ending jungle,
Hiding the hurt, hiding the pain,
Hiding the tears that fall like rain,
Do you realise what you've done?
You've gotten mad and made fun,
How much more can I take,
Constantly trying not to break,
Do you realise I'm human too?
Just like your friends and just like you,
I am the voice of those afraid to speak,
Those who can't because they're too weak,
Do you realise?

Tamzin Anne Wenden (12)
Diss High School, Diss

GROWING UP

Growing up is not that easy
Growing up is hard,
You go through different emotions:
Anger, happiness, frustration and stress
Imagination crumbles and games become less.
Growing up means change
Growing up means feelings.
Choices are crucial
They bring happiness or tears,
Growing up means trying
Growing up means hard work
Practice makes perfect
So, learn from your mistakes.
Growing up means getting better
Growing up means taking chances.
Opportunities come
Take them while you can.
Growing up means losing
Growing up means gain,
You lose friends along the way
For better or for worse
Growing up means regret
Growing up is a challenge!
So bring it on.

Libby Wynn-Fraine (13)
Diss High School, Diss

WAR!

The heroes of war
They walk our streets
Live in our villages
We may never know them
But we see them
Just as civilians
Just as people
We may not know their stories
We may not know their fear
We live in a world that they serve
We live in a world that they save
They risk their lives every day
They lose people they serve with
They lose people they live with
Yet they carry on
Yet they keep fighting
And yet we are knowledgeless
We have not helped
We have not saved
We do not know their stories
We do not know their fear
We do not even notice
The heroes of war are here.

Mia Somers (13)
Diss High School, Diss

STOCK CAR

What is it, you might ask?
A game?
American?
No!

Stock car is when nothing else matters
Waiting for that green flag to fly
All or nothing
That's stock car

A whole week of work up the yard
Just for the weekend
Blood, sweat and tears
That's stock car

A family thing where everyone goes
Just for the weekend
A van and trailer or a lorry
That's stock car

Something you pick up a knack for
from one generation to another
A sixth sense
That's stock car

The champion
David Aldous
Better than the rest

A record holder
Four world championship finals
That's what stock car is.

Alfie Aldous (12)
Diss High School, Diss

MY BROTHER, JOE

Why did you have to go?
You could have stayed longer.

Those motorbikes take lives, lives of innocent people
And now you're with the angels.

You were my idol, my best friend
But the moment you were gone
My life changed for the worst.

You didn't have to leave us
You had a heart of gold.

Joe, we miss you so much
We know it won't happen but
Please walk back through that door
And tell us you're okay
Please come back, Joe.

But now you're gone, gone forever.
See you soon, brother of mine.
I send my prayers.

Rosie Reeve (13)
Diss High School, Diss

HISTORY

H enry's wives divorced, beheaded, died, divorced,
beheaded and survived.
I ndustrial Revolution - this created the steam powered
boat and factories.
S oldiers fought for justice and peace in World War One
and Two.
T he Declaration of Right of men was formed in France
and
O thers saw England win the 1966 World Cup, or perhaps
saw the 1666 Great Fire of London.
R eal lives were harmed and destroyed because of pain
and suffering.
Y ou have been in the world of history, power, freedom
and people.

Callum Doe (12)
Diss High School, Diss

WHY?

Why is school so boring?
Every single lesson I'm yawning,
Why does everyone think they're cool?
When they really look like a fool,
Why am I so bad at games?
I guess I never remember the names,
Why are emojis at the top of the range?
I think we need to make a change,
Why does Spanish always get you down?
It always makes everyone frown,
Why do all the girls flirt with the boys?
When really they prefer to play with their toys,
I guess I will never know,
I'm off to play in the snow.

Lydia May Tatum (12)
Diss High School, Diss

CANCER

First it chooses its victim,
Then it starts to grow,
It chisels and chews away at the body
Going to and fro,
Every year it takes hundreds of innocent lives,
Leaving families lost and grieving.

Last year it took my nan so suddenly,
Leaving me scared and heartbroken,
I cried myself to sleep every night,
Knowing she put up a big fight.

That's why we need your help,
To fight the evil demon,
From taking any more lives!

Erin Gibson (12)
Diss High School, Diss

WHERE HAVE ALL THE CHILDREN GONE?

One day, the children started to go missing.
No one knows where they went
They wandered in the woods
and never returned
Where have all the children gone?

They go to the park
and don't go home
They try to go in their beds
But they are not alone
Where have all the children gone?

The villagers wonder
Where all the children are
they say to each other they can't have gone far
Where have all the children gone?

Rosa Bushell (13)
Diss High School, Diss

WHY

Why do you hate me so much?
I try and look good every day,
But you don't appreciate it.

Is it my hair?
Is it my face?
Is it the way I dress?

Why do I look up to you?
You used to talk to me all the time,
But now you just ignore me.

Why should I keep trying?
You don't look anyway,
It's a waste of my time.

It's just me,
I don't care anymore,
Why did I try? I'm done.

Elli Gipson (12)
Diss High School, Diss

THE WONKY DONKEY

The wonky donkey is wonky
but seems to be quite swanky.
The fleas, he has a ton,
but friends? He has none.

Wonky Donkey lives on his own
No one to contact, no one to phone
Why does nobody like him?
He isn't ugly, fat or thin.

The wonky donkey went clubbing one night,
He found a pony that he liked.
After a lovely date
He found out the name of his mate,
The moany pony.

Benjamin Felix Filmer (13)
Diss High School, Diss

PUPPIES YOU ARE SO CUTE

Puppies, aren't they cute?
They also make people salute
Known as family
Puppies make me jump with glee
When I watch you
I go, "Woohoo!"
We go for long walks
And have long talks
We have fun together
And have a blunder
We wear each other out
Without a doubt
We play outside
With your ball
Then comes nightfall
And our fun is finished with.

Emily Greenacre (12)
Diss High School, Diss

KING CALLUM

King Callum lives in his castle
Until one day, when he receives a parcel
The parcel said, 'Don't try to hide',
So King Callum took a look inside.
He then said, "Ronald!
Let's get a McDonald's!"
Ronald said "Why?"
"I've got coupons for life!"

Finn Wilcockson (13)
Diss High School, Diss

MUM AND DAD

Mum and Dad are so great,
Like when we hug and paint
Mum and Dad are so cool,
Even when I win at pool.

Mum and Dad, I love you lots,
When I'm in trouble they untangle the knots
Blood is red, the sky is blue,
All I can say to you is
Mum and Dad, I love you.

Callum Harris (13)
Diss High School, Diss

DANCING IN THE RAIN

Black clouds above bellow loud,
Soft raindrops waltz down from the clouds,
Lightning shoots across the sky,
No sun in sight way up high,
The trees are being thrown around,
Only me to hear the sounds,
Beneath the skies you feel no pain,
Come, dance with me out in the rain.

Naomi Ely (13)
Diss High School, Diss

THE FIGHT FOR FEMINISTS

We are told, you are too young to be a feminist,
Yet no one is too young to be sexist,
So, I congratulate the world on its controversy,
For underestimating what I - a woman, can achieve.

Women; judged by style over substance
Inner beauty has no value, just what is seen at first glance,
Barbie doll beauty - no blemishes; who are you to dictate?
Not too tall, size four clothes and a perfect, petit waist.

Society tells us this little world is perfect,
Yet women still aren't shown enough respect,
Rather than branding them with a number out of ten,
You should be praising our women every now and again.

They say: boys like you better when you wear make-up,
Plastic surgery and hair extensions, all for the fake love,
Short skirts; tight dresses; thin thighs; pretty eyes,
Women conceal their imperfections, always hidden in disguise.

So I ask you now, why do people despise feminists?
For fighting with their words and not their fists,
Why do we abuse them and exclude them from society?
When feminists fight for what *all* women should be.

Sian Freestone (13)
Litcham School, Litcham

YOU KNEW...

All you heard was the shouting of her violent dad,
You knew if you weren't in her house, you were to be glad,
You never saw her tear up,
As she covered her scars with make-up,
But you did nothing.

They bullied her in the hall,
Because she was too tall,
Or her breasts were too small,
Just because they wanted to show off and act cool,
But you did nothing.

But you knew they were only a small part of the reason she cried inside,
You knew all she wanted to do was hide,
You know she couldn't because everywhere she went she was abused,
And everywhere she went she was accused,
But you did nothing.

She was accused for being herself and she was constantly bruised,
Just so that her father was amused,
Her legs were always red,
And her arms always bled,
But you did nothing.

You knew she didn't want all the neglect,
You knew she just wanted someone who would protect,
You knew she was constantly in pain,
You knew the stains weren't pen, but bloodstains,
But you did nothing.

And that's why she didn't make it to her teens,
Because no one listened to her screams,
So no one called 999,
Because they all thought she was fine,
But you did nothing.

And you knew,
You knew but you thought no one would think it was true,
And now you feel a great load of contrite,
And now you know child abuse isn't right.

So now you speak out,
And you tell everyone to speak out,
Because no one should ever have a doubt,
Everyone should speak out.

Not because you loved her,
But because child abuse isn't right!

Ella Westhorpe (13)
Litcham School, Litcham

MY FEARS

I'm not your usual girl that cares what they wear
On an everyday basis, with long, styled hair.
I don't cake my face whenever I need to go
Out into the big world. It's fine,
That, I know.

I'll wear trainers, a hat, a hoodie and jeans,
Carry a bag with a million Jelly Beans.
Eyeliner and concealer, eyeshadow and gloss
Nothing more than to hide the sleep that
I've lost.

But people don't agree, they laugh and they shout
Towards me, no one helps while I cry out.
The points and the stares from people, young and old
Asking who does she think she is?
She thinks that
She's bold.

I don't want the figure that everyone wishes to see
Curved, skinny and nice: It doesn't feel like me.
Soft edges and lines blend in way too far
Become much of the norm, stay under that
Society bar.

My body doesn't feel as if I fit in here
People assume who I am from far and from near.

Of course, people laugh again and again for that
You look amazing, a girl, deal with that,
It's a fact.

I'm a 'girl', you're a boy. It works well for some,
But for me, not so much, my insides feel numb.
With your words and laughs, you've tired me out.
I can't give a damn. I can't even shout.
I'm not what you think, but no one will hear,
That I'm not a girl nor a boy, so hide that
jeer.

Listen now when I say
No one will hear
A shout of an in-betweener
Of a trans kid's fears.

Kyra Pugh (15)
Litcham School, Litcham

A FRIEND WITH DEPRESSION

I realise you think you're hopeless,
I know you feel meaningless,
But you're worth a great deal to me,
I'm here for you.

You think nobody cares for you,
You reckon nobody talks to you,
I listen to your doubts,
I'm here for you.

The thoughts you have,
Make you suffer,
I can help stop them,
I'm here for you.

You don't have to live in fear,
You should be able to tell everyone,
Your life will get better,
I'm here for you.

When everything is kept in,
But you need to let it out,
Talk to me,
I'm here for you.

You don't seem needy,
You're not going to be judged,
You are not the only one,
I'm here for you.

You can't cry,
Because your tears feel like acid,
So speak up,
I'm here for you.

When your mind is like a gloomy day,
And you feel snowed in,
Come and find me,
I'm here for you.

If you can't see the horizon,
Or the rainbow in the sky,
You don't need to worry,
I'm here for you.

Something has gone wrong,
You can't do anything about it,
You feel like it's your fault,
I'm here for you.

If you're known as the geek,
If you're known as the wimp,
Destroy the words,
I'm here for you.

Help a friend with depression,
You could save them,
With four simple words,
I'm here for you.

Isla Palmer (13)
Litcham School, Litcham

TWINS

Being a twin is not as they say
We are different in every single way.
This poem should help others to know
That some twins won't wear each other's clothes
We haven't got superpowers, if only I did
Then I would turn invisible if I could
To disappear from the world
When someone says, "What lovely girls,
Are they twins?" they always say.
No, really? We just look the same.

"Which one are you?"
"Please just go away!"
"Nobody likes the good twin!" they say.
"We like your twin better than you,"
"Do you hate her? Cause she hates you!"
"She is better and smarter than you, don't you see?"
They're trying to compare my sister and me!

Well I love my sister
I don't care what they say
I'm five minutes older anyway.

Lily May Bygrave (12)
Litcham School, Litcham

WORDS HURT

She was not made to be like them.
Not with their long, shiny hair,
nor their skinny waists and thigh gaps,
Or their perfect olive skin,
She was made to look different.

She wasn't made like them.
Not with their size-four figures,
Nor their white teeth and dimpled smiles,
Or even their long lashes and perfectly shaped brows,
She was made to look different.

So this one girl at school decided to point that out.
Decided to point out that she didn't have that long hair,
Or that amazing, skinny body,
that she was 'different'
'ugly'
'worthless'

With bottled-up emotions,
She suddenly wasn't hungry anymore,
She'd sit in her room alone and make herself sick,
She'd look at her bathroom scales at her feet,
and cry. Sit by the door with bloodshot eyes.

Day to day,
She suddenly started wearing long-sleeved tops,
And only came downstairs for dinner.
Nobody questioned why,
Nobody even noticed.

Until that day, on her 15th birthday,
Everyone started to care, just a little too late,
She was in the bath for around seven hours,
Water filled the landing and flooded down the stairs,
When someone who just started to care,
Opened the door.
Opened it to a flooded room,
And no one else's heart beating but the person's who started to care
a little too late.

Sophia Djiakouris (14)
Litcham School, Litcham

FREEDOM

My freedom is my gift
There's so much I can do
Like ride a bike and go to school
They're not the only two

I am not forced to work or marry young
My mum just wants me to have fun
I don't worship a god who mandates death
Or spew learned hatred with every breath

Mum says I need to live my life
To learn, to play and grow
To run in the sun
Dance in the rain
And make angels in the snow

To have some dreams
And make them true
Just be happy, be me, in all I do
Often I stop and realise
And hear stories from other places
Girls forced to live in silent pain
No freedom, no voices, no faces

Made to marry, not allowed to be
A child, have fun, to ever see

The person that could have laughed and grown
No time for that, life's not their own

Forced to marry for a family's honour
A man so old he's almost a goner
Or made to work for 10p a day
For a cup of grain, no time to play

A voice is silenced, no one hears
All her hopes and all her fears
They're pushed aside, out of reach
It's taken away
The freedom of speech

Am I grateful for the life I have?
You better believe I am
One day I'll use my voice for others
That's *my* freedom, my gift...
And I can.

Rhiannon Bell (12)
Litcham School, Litcham

THE BRIGHT BLUE HIJAB

Boom, the bomb goes off
Word spreading like a cold or a cough
As she walks down the street, people whisper
They stare, she hears words in her ear
"Look out, run away, beware,"
What is anyone running from?

The Paris attack was last week
Now she's yet again 'a terrorist freak'
I'll have you know, she has never hurt a soul
Never ever been mean, never lost control

Pray for Paris, they say
For the world we should pray
She has been here now for three years
Now she's the face of everyone's fears

But is it her face, or merely the cloth?
A rectangle of material, that last week was ripped off
By some racist, closed minded, idiotic critter
Who continued to cuss, scream, shout and hit her

If you were to ask me who I would be scared of
I would tell you the man
Who attacked an innocent refugee from Iran

Who assumed because a woman wore a hijab
That she was a terrorist
Her injuries stopped her from making it to work that day
She was one step away, just one step away
One step away from curing cancer in the lab

But the man, he couldn't see past the bright blue hijab.

Amy Williams (15)
Litcham School, Litcham

OURSELVES

Others view us as,
Liars, cheats, bullies, idiots,
Friends, family, relatives,
Life, death, strength,
Others view us as,
Dumb, stupid,
Selfless, confident, annoying,
Dark, light and everything in-between.

We see ourselves as,
Good, bad,
Dumb, stupid, idiots,
Life, death,
We view ourselves as
Old, young,
Silly, strong, sensible,
Fat, thin

We want to be viewed as,
Strong, fit, athletic,
Smart, funny, cute,
Life, light, love,
We want to be viewed as,
Friends, family,
Young, youthful,
Useful in many ways

We see ourselves as,
Good, bad,
Dumb, stupid, idiots,
Life, death,
We view ourselves as,
Old, young,
Silly, strong, sensible,
Fat, thin,

Does it even matter?
Whether we are fat, thin,
Old, young,
Strong, weak?
Does it matter?
We are different and unique,
In all different ways,
So don't judge on appearance or race,
Don't judge at all,
We are who we are,
And we can't change our face,
Does it even matter how others view us?
It is about how we view ourselves
Does it even matter?

Jack Babey (13)
Litcham School, Litcham

RECOGNITION

People see me as intelligent, though I am still not recognised.
People see me as talented, but they do not take me seriously.
People see me as friendly, however they do not understand why.

You see, truth is, I'm nothing.
I see myself as nothing.
I see just another shadow in the mirror.
It stares at me blankly.
I stare back.
I use my 'talents' to make myself recognised.
I use my 'intelligence' to make myself recognised.
I am 'friendly' to make myself recognised.
However, no matter how hard I try,
I still see myself as just another shadow.

When I am alone, I feel as if I will be like that
For the rest of my life.
Miserable,
Cold,
Dead.
This is all because I don't have recognition.
How do the others do it? I would ask myself.
How do the others get recognised,
Greeted by friendly cheers and happy smiles?

But the answer is obvious.
I am not intelligent.
I am not talented.
I am not friendly.
That's what they all say to make me happy.
But the truth is...
...They all are...
And that is why I'm not recognised...

Alice Kathleen Crisp (13)
Litcham School, Litcham

COEXIST

Why can't we coexist,
Just a little bit,
Sometimes I can't bear,
To look at the world, it gives me a scare,
All of the hate,
Flying around, spread by people wanting us to take the bait,
They want to make us sad,
Make us mad,
So we become bad.

Why can't we coexist,
Just a little bit?
Why do we discriminate?
Why are our hearts filled with hate?
Why do we hate things that are different?
Are we ignorant?
Unable to escape our own views
Does everything have to be aligned, like church pews?
We should dare to be different,
Or is that incoherent
To your ideology?
We need to escape from this hateful monotony
Of treating people differently because of their anatomy
Or if they have different-coloured skin
We treat them like a bin
To pour our discriminatory messages into

And there's more
All this hate is like a sore,
Infecting the planet, I'm bored
Of it, we're forever fighting,
Like two dogs biting,
Oh, why can't we coexist just a little bit?

Felix Platt (13)
Litcham School, Litcham

WHY?

I have watched forests grow,
I have seen mountains fall.
I have watched humanity form over many,
many years,
I have seen the most beautiful things,
of which you can only dream.
I walk the deserts,
I fly the skies,
I conquer the mountains,
I swim the deep,
I slide along the icy glades,
I master the art
of overcoming the world.
Whilst I own the wild
and tackle my life...
you take it all away.

You pollute my oceans.
You take away my forests.
You kill my family,
for no common reason.
You build your homes
where mine once was.
You disturb my peace
with your noisy machines.

You take away my food,
and drive away my friends.
You never seem to understand,
and never seem
to cease poisoning my land.
Why do you need
to cause such decay?
Why does everything
have to go your way?
Why can you not just understand?
Why do you make such desolation
your job?
And why...
Why do you always close the door,
that we opened before you?

Emily Claire Jones (12)
Litcham School, Litcham

CURVES

Fat, chubby, greedy, round
Wrong
Curvacious

My friends see me as
A curvy person
My foes see me as
A pig
My family see me as
A rounded person
No one cares for what I
See me as
They say I'm
Fat, I eat too much, have too many curves
Curvy, they only focus on my chest not my heart
Weird, why do I hide my body?

But
I see myself as so much more
Fierce, I won't show if I'm breaking
A tiger, my stretch marks just show my stripes
Empowered, I'm strong and won't let the hurt show
No one knows the *real* me

So what?
These words don't affect me
Or at least that's what they think

Really, I'm screaming on the inside
I say the words don't hurt but they go to my head
Filling me with dread...

So what?
My smile is acting like a mask
So what?
The days I say I'm busy, I'm really crying
So what?
I hate my body but love it at the same time
So what?
What now?

Elana-Rose Lilley (13)
Litcham School, Litcham

SHE WAS ONLY THIRTEEN

She was only thirteen,
When her friend pointed out that she wasn't perfect,
And she wasn't the stick-thin model that everyone else was,
She was 'fat',

She was only thirteen,
When her mum caught her not eating,
She would throw away meals,
And pretend she was full,

She was only thirteen,
When she forgot about her health,
And focussed only on her figure,
To look like everyone else,

She was only thirteen,
When she sat in her bathroom,
Alone, hours on end, crying,
About the numbers at her feet,

She was only thirteen,
When she no longer revealed her arms,
Scared of the comments about her scars,
But they were true, that is what she had done

She was only thirteen,
When she took her own life,
Lying awake every night,
She just wanted the pain to go,

She was only thirteen,
When her parents found her,
Alone in the cold,
Sitting in silence,

She didn't even make it to fourteen.

Aimee Paige Wright (13)
Litcham School, Litcham

MOTHER

You always said nobody wanted me
All you ever did was neglect me
You made me feel all alone
But perhaps if you'd have shown

The world in a different light
A home that would keep me safe at night
Warm, open arms that would welcome me
Then maybe you wouldn't have to see

My coffin being carried forward
Through a sea of sorrowed faces
But you're all probably now celebrating
Because you no longer have to continue with your hating

As for me, I'm safe now
In Heaven I cannot be abused
Those bruises and scars that cover my body
Are nothing more than a terrible story

But don't think that's okay, mother,
Everything you did was wrong.
Because I never spoke out,
Is now the reason that I'll never shout

You are a cruel and heartless criminal
All you ever did was abuse me.

Sitting in this church today should give you the sign
That you are the reason, that my life was never mine.

Danielle Mia Harrowing (14)
Litcham School, Litcham

SHE IS BLACK AND I AM WHITE

Just a few years ago I believed
That everything was right in the world,
In my little, comfortable cocoon.
But growing up,
And breaking out,
I began to see
I am lucky to be this free...
But I know the power of words:

You call her an abomination,
I say that's discrimination.
You spit in her face,
Because of her race.
As you call her a disgrace,
But she's too scared to file a case.
Your feelings of superiority,
Are rejected by the vast majority;
Who know the power of words.

Not everything is black and white,
And we won't go down without a fight.
There's a whole spectrum of people
Standing up for what is right
How come you can't see the light?

Young people paving the way to equality,
Yet you are still trying to build a wall
To stop the path of equal for all.
You simply say forget about equal rights!
She is black and I am white.

Ayla Freij-Nichols (15)
Litcham School, Litcham

THE MONSTERS

Birds swoop high
above the caged home of the woods
Free, safe from any harm
Well, what will happen when the monsters,
the hunters, come and chop them down?
Where will they go?
What can they do?...

The axe hangs at his waist ready to kill
To kill an aspect of life
to damage the future of the forest
Round it swings, high in the sky
suddenly stabbing the hard, blistering skin
where it bleeds a yellow blood

Down falls the large giant, peacefully lying
never to feel the wind in it's leaves
dead on the ground

The monsters strike again and again
killing the land, the nature we love
But who are these monsters?

That's easy. They are us.
We are the destroyers
our beautiful landscapes ravaged

Who have we become?
Visionaries?
Creators?
Monsters or hunters?
Just think.
How did we become this...?

Ellen Stringer (11)
Litcham School, Litcham

DREAMS

I want to be a professional dancer on Strictly,
Whoever sniggers at me,
And my glorious dream,
They will just wait and see.

I want to be a professional dancer on Strictly,
With the training I'll be gaining in order to be divine,
With this,
I shall shine.

I want to be a professional dancer on Strictly,
Glamour and grace,
Not yet,
Sequins and sparkle,
Not yet,
Elegance and pace,
Not yet,
These will come in time,
So one day,
It will be showtime.

I want to be a professional dancer on Strictly,
My cousin wants to be an author,
My sister wants to act in a Harry Potter spin-off,
My friend wants to be a performer,
These aren't traditional jobs or dreams,
But anything is achievable if you believe.

I want to be a professional dancer on Strictly,
What about you?
Believe in it,
And anything can come true!

Courtney Burton (15)
Litcham School, Litcham

EVERY DAY

Failure.
Do you ever feel like this?
Expectancy weighing you down,
Pressure pulling you apart.
Are you good enough? Do you make a difference?
Does anyone care?
Millions of people around the world feel like this.
Every day.
Pushed past in the corridor.
Every day.
Ignored like you are not even in the room.
Every day.
Friends pretending to be your friend.
Every day.
Insignificant.
Friends gossiping behind your back,
Secrets bouncing off the walls.
Worthless, never good enough, always someone better.
Snapchat and Instagram showing pictures of people
hanging out - never one with you.
The sleepless nights you face on a pillow of anxiety
And no one cares. The sleepless nights
Crying yourself to sleep, as taunting voices smother,
Never, never realising you weren't the only one.

Emily King (16) & Billie
Litcham School, Litcham

IMAGINE

Imagine you were insane,
Well, in the eyes of other people anyway,
You were just as normal as them,
But had no way to express that.

Imagine you were scared to go to school,
You weren't getting the proper education you needed,
All because of bullying,
On your appearance, way you act and the way you think.

Imagine you were the bully,
You would feel powerful and great,
But inside you think what they could be going through,
And how much you really have hurt them.

Imagine you had no one,
No one to look up to,
No one to express your problems too,
No one to... ugh.

Just image how you would feel to be that person,
Having no one on your side,
Friends ganging up on you,
Family thinking you're insane,
Non-stop stress.

Just imagine...

Matthew Wells (12)
Litcham School, Litcham

YOUR STORY

A book is a portal,
To a far-off land,
It could be of a desert filled with hot sand,
Could be with mountains, with snow so deep,
Could be a castle with a dungeon and keep,
All these stories are revived once more,
Read to children from the age of four.

Some books are filled with emotion,
With happiness and fear,
Some can make you laugh out loud,
And some to shed a tear,
You are getting older now,
It will soon be your time to go,
To make your mark on the world,
And have children of your own.

Some stories stick with you forever,
Even when you're wise and old,
When your children have grandchildren,
Those stories can still be told.

What about your story,
The life that you have led?
A story that can be retold,
A story that can be read.

Ruby Elizabeth Bygrave (12)
Litcham School, Litcham

WINTER!

Of all the seasons in the year
Winter is my favourite.

I like the fact there could be snow
and the good fun we have,
Snowball fights, making snowmen,
Sleigh rides are a few
Of the things I like to do.

The crunchy sound of the snow as you're walking,
The cloud of vapour when we're talking.

The cosy nights by the fire,
With a hot chocolate warming our hands,
The things we look forward to.

Such bonfire night with fireworks
And warming soup and baked potatoes,
Writing names with sparklers.
And there's Christmas as well,
My favourite type of holiday,
The excitement of presents gets me overwhelmed,
And there's also the family gatherings.

These are the reasons why
Winter is my favourite season.

Dylan Downes (13)
Litcham School, Litcham

UNHAPPINESS

Grieving our losses,
Losing our heart,
Saying farewell,
As we break apart.

Death is ultimate,
Darkening pain,
Losing our loved ones,
Never seen again.

Sad and bad,
It makes you cry,
To hide tears,
You must lie.

A place never filled,
But a heartbeat away,
The ones you truly love,
Never go away.

But life goes on,
And now it's time to rest,
Although their time is over,
They have had the best.

Tears of sadness,
Remind you of the love

Covering you with happiness,
And memories from above.

Death and being born are the only two things guaranteed in life,
And love is the stuff in-between,
The stuff that gives you a life of happiness,
The stuff that everyone has seen.

Jessica Banham (13)
Litcham School, Litcham

EQUESTRIANS

You asked me what sport I do
I said I am an Equestrian
You said
That's not a sport
It's easy
It requires no skill at all
All you do is sit there
It's harmless
Little did you know the words you were speaking
were misguided
To be be an equestrian you require
Sportsmanship
Tolerance
Skill
Balance
Strength
Passion
Courage
Commitment
Persistence
Do you finally understand that riding
Is not just a sport, it's also and extreme passion
The risk we take in order to succeed
And do the thing we love is outstanding

Equestrians are people
People that should be very much respected
And there is nothing else in the world that can ever even come close
To comparing against the feeling of riding a horse.

Grace Fisher (11)
Litcham School, Litcham

MY FAMILY

Family's so strong and happy,
Helping each other through
the tough and through the painful.

Everyone getting together and having fun,
Brothers, sisters, finally getting along,
While your mum, dad, friends and other family
are talking where they belong.
So we get to the good bit, that I'm working on.

We start with Dad, the best dad I could ever wish for,
Through the rough and the tough, he is there for me,
When I am sad or angry,
he is there for me.
I love him so much, and that is a thank you from me.

Now Mum, the mum of my dreams,
Looking for people and she chose me!
When we first made contact, I knew she loved me.
This poem I made for you and me,
When I think of family, I think of all we could be.

Toby Chestney (13)
Litcham School, Litcham

A DAY AT THE ZOO

Walking down a corridor of depression
With it twisting and turning through anger and hate,
Yet I still hear myths about the Great Confession
Where the zombies will decide the animals' fate.
Thousands of brainless beings that aren't empathic,
And they refuse to admit that their lives are pathetic.

A massive prison that towers above Mother Nature
And the zombies exterminating them by the million,
But at the same time the inmates denature
And the zombies don't turn any more civilian.
I can just stare at the hopelessness in their eyes,
The knowing that they will never achieve life's prize.

As I leave from my day at the zoo,
I wonder, *say if we were the animals,*
and the animals were me and you.

Issac Bower (14)
Litcham School, Litcham

LOST VOICES

People go missing every day,
Who knows whether they'll come back today.
Families are torn apart,
Trying to make a new start.

Tears are shed,
Their loved ones, dead.
Others are stressed,
Even more are depressed.

Our world is a cruel place,
You can go missing without a trace.
Children and adults scream,
And cling onto their only dream.

One day they wish to be found,
So they can return home safe and sound.
They're beaten, tortured and abused,
They're punished, tormented and bruised.

Unfortunately some will never be found again,
As they sadly die in horrific pain.
These are the lost voices of people who'll never be free,
The innocent and deceased ones we will never see.

Evelyn Scott (13)
Litcham School, Litcham

A DIFFERENT PERCEPTIVE

Who am I?
Thinking, breathing, walking, dreaming, that's me
I am the fire that just keeps burning,
I am a storm, living, learning.

I am time now and later, I am youth, and I am nature
I am a lion, brave and strong, listening, waiting, on and on
I am water, clear as day
I am love, growing day by day.

I am silence, dead and still,
I am a secret, ready to spill,
I'm a nightmare, I'm a dream
I'm a king, I am a queen.

I am your fear, angry and harsh
I am a field filled with fresh grass
I am wisdom, with knowledge galore,
I am interesting, never a bore

Well, I hope I answered your question,
The one from before
Now answer my question
Who are you?

Maisy Jones (13)
Litcham School, Litcham

A LONELY TREE

I am just a lonely tree,
I am at an old age,
I am now free,
I will turn a new page.

I look really old,
As heavy as a shelf,
As I got told,
I can't think to myself.

A lonely tree,
Should never be alone,
A tree who is free,
Should find his favourite zone.

I have connected with other trees,
But now I am lonely,
Many trees have had their frees,
I am going very slowly.

I have flowed through lots,
My brain is now heavy,
I feel like a pot,
That just has one memory.

I feel like an empty tin,
I would like a new life,
Some of my memories have been put in a bin,
Maybe I would like a wife.

William Taylor (13)
Litcham School, Litcham

POLICEMEN

Where would we be without policemen?
Anarchy, chaos, mayhem;
explosions, fires, guns, drugs, robberies, murders,
No way of peace.

When policemen complete their training they take an oath
To uphold the laws and serve and protect.
Every day they stop a tiny part of the world
Falling into chaos
and keep everybody safe.

But even though they do all that, people don't care,
Call them pigs and other offensive terms,
Unaware of what they're doing for everybody.

They are smart, brave, courageous,
Fast, strong, good in armed and unarmed combat,
And are able to think on their feet.
Where would we be without policemen?

Jake Linney (11)
Litcham School, Litcham

THE WORLD WE LIVE IN

Morning light, streaks of cloud,
Creatures of the night no longer make a sound.
Blue sky, pink light,
The morning is a beautiful sight.

Trees bare, creeping in,
The silhouettes of the world we live in.
Iced over, puddles deep,
Is it worth our loss of sleep?

Rolling hills, painted green,
We do not know what lies unseen,
The sun rises, do not grieve,
It's a shadow of the future we cannot perceive.

Vapour trails paint the sky,
The world illuminated by the street lights,
Puddles formed in the ruts of machines,
Which are used to decimate the trees.

These are the silhouettes of the world we live in.

Katie Louise Heffer (14)
Litcham School, Litcham

WHO OR WHAT?

The trees were shadowing me,
Slicing any light that remained.
The night was dark and dismal.
The rain was hitting me like cannonballs,
I could hear the slight rustle in the leaves.
Then something much more spooky
Whispered.
It was faint at first,
But grew louder with every second that passed.
All of a sudden, two red eyes flicked on and off.
I turned and ran.
I could hear the leaves rustling behind me.
But then, silence, followed by an unexpected,
Deathly shriek.
I carried on running.
Stumbling over roots.
But then something much bigger,
A dead body.
I shrieked
To find something big charging my way.

Ollie Johnson (11)
Litcham School, Litcham

THE FUTURE

The future is described as a black hole,
The unknown, the oblivion or a haunted house,
We should be scared of it is what they say.

People say they're scared of the future,
That when they imagine it,
All they see is black,
People say they don't know what's coming,
And that they don't want it,
They're all wrong.

We shouldn't be afraid of it,
That we should see black and white,
Excitement and fear,
And it's true,
The future is a blank page,
A positive page!

We define the future,
We hold the pen,
We change the future,
Don't let the future change you!

George Harrison (12)
Litcham School, Litcham

I CAN'T WRITE POEMS

I can't write poems because I don't think they are important.
I guess you could say it's full of nothing, so it's unimportant.
People tell me it's full of emotion, really,
There has to be another solution.
Please can someone just come up with a better evolution?
People say poems are great
But trying to come up with one is not an easy fate.
Can't people just come up with
Something better than a poem,
Like just a weird story?
I bet if someone made something better,
There would be some glory.
So this is why I can't make a poem
I think it's a waste of time,
So now you know, stop making me rhyme.

Aiden Mackney (12)
Litcham School, Litcham

EQUAL RIGHTS

Less money, why? Less jobs, why?
Pretty pink dresses and frilly scarves
Is this being a girl?
What about equal pay? No? Why?
Because of our gender.
What about more job options? No? Why?
Because of our gender.
Men are better, stronger, braver.
What about women who are better, stronger, braver?
No? Why?
Because we're girls.
Is it fair? No.
Is it just? No.
Will it continue if we don't do something about it?
Yes.
No more sexism.
It's not fair, just or true. But it will continue.
No more sexism.
You could be the one that changes everything.
Stop sexism now before it's too late...

Ruby Alana Burton (12)
Litcham School, Litcham

WHY STRIVE?

Why strive for more when we are content with what we are?
Why strive to not change when the world can be explored?
Why fight for gods when they bear no mercy?
Why fight for men when they lie and cheat?
Why build when it's only destroyed?
Why build when it's only a pile of stone?
Why bear children when they are doomed to your fate?
Why bear children if they'll start the cycle again?

We strive for the imperfect perfection
We strive for the future of us
We care for your culture
We care for our culture
We dare to make our meaning whatever we want it
We dare to live
We dare to care
You are human.

Finley Barnes (13)
Litcham School, Litcham

WE ARE WHAT WE ARE

We are what we are
Because we're all different
Some have freckles, some don't,
Some have ginger hair, some don't,
Everyone thinks differently, not the same
We're all different

We are what we are
Because some are tall, some are short,
Some are bullied, some are bullies,
Some laugh, some cry,
We're all different.

We are what we are
Because some are happy, some are sad
Some delight in others suffering, others don't
We're all different.

We are what we are
Because some are young, some are old,
Some learn, and some don't,
We're all different.

James David Tuckwell (13)
Litcham School, Litcham

ASPIRE TO INSPIRE

Aspire to be your better self,
To become like your idol,
To gain trophies on your shelf,
Aspire towards your sense of pride.

Motivate yourself to achieve,
To do one better than yourself,
To have an ace up your sleeve,
Motivate to create.

Inspire, don't aspire,
To inspire others and not yourself,
To stoke your motivational fire
Inspire others to aspire to be like you.

Men can move mountains,
It can take time,
To reach out and obtain,
The flame that drives you.

Nothing is impossible,
The word itself says,
"I'm possible"
As Audrey Hepburn said.

Ben Druce (14)
Litcham School, Litcham

MY MUM'S NEW BOYFRIEND

Used, pushed, shoved out the way,
This is what I feel like every day,
"Home sweet home," so they say

Abused, tortured, hit,
My mum doesn't realise one bit,
My life, I want to commit

School, school, school
Maybe it's good, maybe it's not
The names I get called; there's quite a lot
In any games, I get forgot,
At least it's better than my lot

I get a nice welcome of shouting when I step through the door,
He spends all our money on drinks, that's why we're so poor,
My mum doesn't ever ensure I'm secure,
I just have to endure.

Ella Stonebanks (13)
Litcham School, Litcham

A DIFFERENT PERSPECTIVE

England is so boring, as boring as its rainy days,
There's never any sunshine, only filth and grain,
People say we're posh, shooting wildlife,
But really we're not posh, we just like living life.

The capitals are dirty, filled with grey days
People are so talkative, you can never get away,
The roads are never smooth, unlike your highways,
The potholes are so dangerous, waiting for their prey.

Really, England isn't that bad, as bad as you would think,
It's really just the rumours, like jam being spread on bread,
Just like I did at the beginning of my verse.

Joshua James Carter (13)
Litcham School, Litcham

HUMAN PLAYING GOD

We have answers but no questions
They think they can explain
It's a subject, impossible to imagine
Life after death is an impossible struggle
Eternity may eat our souls
We think we are mere mortals
But we will never publicly know
How long is a piece of string?

Infinity has overcome the mind
A plague to our lack of knowledge
It's sad how one of our biggest fears
Is something we can't explain
We are jealous of what we don't know
Is this just a fear of omniscience?
Are we just too afraid to admit
We are scared of what lies within?

Reuben Gardner (13)
Litcham School, Litcham

WHY DO WE COMPLAIN?

Why do we complain,
When we are really not in pain?
When we have food and a family,
Even if you think you're not happy.

Just think of those in therapy,
Whether it's chemo or mental,
When what life they have left is fierce,
And not at all gentle,
Just imagine thinking at night,
If in the morning you would've lost the fight.

Just think of those without a roof over their head,
Without clean water and any sort of bed,
Hopefully one day we'll realise,
Our lives are as good as they should be,
When we complain, we are being weak.

Jim Massey (14)
Litcham School, Litcham

HIS STORY

The boy down the road, he never existed,
The people that took his soul were sick and twisted.
His one sister and three brothers,
feel like they have lost him to others.

On the 21st, was when he died,
I know his heart tried to keep him alive.
His mum and dad sat in despair,
They lost their son, does anyone care?

He died in childbirth
He never set foot on this Earth.
He lies asleep, under the ground,
Hoping, one day, he will be found.

His name was Bradley Christopher Thomas Galer,
I am his sister,
And this is his story.

Sophie-Anne Elizabeth Galer (12)
Litcham School, Litcham

ODE TO FAKE NEWS

I will write the truth,
Precise black letters,
Cutting deep,
Roaring whispers of lies,
Selective snipping,
Inner grace,
Pale, spindly,
Fingers that softly scribble...

I will read the truth,
As decreed by deities,
Above me,
Against a tumultuous,
Cycle,
A simple constant,
That remains true,
Eyes that softly read...

I will be the truth,
Shining like a beacon,
Vigilante,
Perception formed,
By truths I know,
Judgement I will pass,
On the dark masses below,
Fists that softly punch...

Amelia Platt (15)
Litcham School, Litcham

WHY DO PEOPLE MISTREAT ANIMALS?

Why do we hurt the ones we love?
For instance animals
Our pals should get treated properly

Poor, defenceless, innocent creatures
Kicked, punched, tortured and mauled
Why do people do it?

Think of a world without people
Hurting and mistreating animals
What would it be like to you?

People are supposed to be kind to animals,
Not mistreating animals in our world
What have they done to you?

Animals are disposable
That's what people think
As they don't see a beating heart
So it is time for a rethink.

Nirvana Marley Box (13)
Litcham School, Litcham

THIS IS ME

I am me, I am free,
I can be who I want to be.
No matter what you say,
I will be me anyway.

I won't lie, I won't hide,
I am free to be me.
Don't be mean, just because you hate my personality.

You don't have to stay and talk to me,
For you could go, be free.
And if you don't like me,
Just go,
Just leave.

I will always be free,
I will always be me.
I think with my heart,
Even when it tears me apart.
I have learned something:
Although it may sting,
I must always be true to me.

Yasmine Knights (12)
Litcham School, Litcham

THE GARDEN OF THOUGHT

The flower of imagination,
Growing in the flower bed of thought,
In the garden of your brain,
With the blossoms of your ideas.

The flower has a voice,
The voice of you,
Say that voice to the world,
Because most of them want to hear it,
Your voice can make a difference.

That flowers grow within us,
We are the gardener,
We trim and prune our imagination,
We limit and we grow.

Others have that flower too,
Just the same as us,
Because we are all the gardeners,
The gardeners of our imagination.

Felix Daniells (13)
Litcham School, Litcham

TIGER

Gargantuan creature,
Ruler of the jungle.
A muscular, orange body,
Patrolling the forest floor.
Dinner-plate paws,
Shuddering tropical surroundings,
Shivering, shaking with each step.
Agile ears,
Detecting every minute movement,
With a fading hope,
Of its next meal.
Curious amber eyes,
Scan the canopy of green above.
A silhouette of a hunter,
His visage dark and reckless.
Barrel pointed menacingly,
Between its panic-stricken eyes.
Blackness...
Like a candle,
Senselessly snuffed out.

Olivia Finlay (12)
Litcham School, Litcham

MISTAKES

Mistakes:
Mistakes are easy to make,
Especially when you're stupid enough
To stay awake till midnight.
Mistakes are easy to redo;
But when you stay awake at night,
Well, that is a very bad thing to do.
You make them more easily,
Then it all turns into a confusing stew.
Everyone makes mistakes,
But especially when you stay awake till midnight.
Mistakes are like a fawn learning to walk;
They get up, then fall down.
That is the mistake that you make;
And then, well, you do it again and again.
Misteak!

Jess Bluebell King (12)
Litcham School, Litcham

OKAY

You hide behind your feelings.
Hide the truth away.
Pretend to be happy and say you're okay.

You say all these words.
But they all make you hurt.
Pretend to be happy and say you're okay.

People say, "Are you alright?"
But you still have to think overnight.
Pretend to be happy and say you're okay.

You finally tell someone.
You feel like you have won.
You say all these words that cheer you up.
The clouds divide and the sun breaks through.
And you feel like brand new.

Keeva Lake (12)
Litcham School, Litcham

ALL ABOUT FAMILY

F unny moments in the past to look back on to make us laugh.
A bout looking after the people around you making sure they are perfect.
M ostly look after the nan and grandad when they get to the tough stage
I always think of my family before me because they mean the most to me
L osing a member is the worst thing you could have done to you but don't stop fighting
Y elling at your family is the worst thing you could do because they also back you up during tough times so you don't want to lose them.

Josh Reeve (13)
Litcham School, Litcham

MIND BEHIND BARS

People lie to fit in a chain,
An endless chain of society,
Twisting their brains.

Twisted brains which eat at their sins,
Just look at them again
And help them win.

Help them win their silent fight,
The one that no one knows,
The one that keeps them up at night.

Nobody knows how she cries to sleep,
Everything everyone says to her,
How they cut so deep.

She goes into school with her mind's fresh scars,
All the feelings she's hiding,
With her mind behind bars.

Roisin Coronin (12)
Litcham School, Litcham

SEASONS

Summer is a lovely time for fires in the garden
The heatwaves not so pleasant

Autumn has pretty gold and brown leaves on the ground
Crackling as you walk on them

Winter is a great time for seeing scenery
All the snow-covered trees and frozen lakes
The crunch of snow beneath your feet

Spring with the fresh smell of grass
And the sight of green covered trees
The lovely red roses
The noise of hedgehogs

The cycle starts again
Another year
Another life
Another poem.

Theoden Hammond (11)
Litcham School, Litcham

THE DECISION

The decision, will it happen?
Or will it be flattened
by the extent of the people?
The decision

The decision, will he button up
the people's free speech or
happen to dictate the country?
The decision

The decision, will we use the
olive branch or the bayonette
to bring the world closer?
The decision

The decision, will she start
the talks to salvage our friendship
with another continent
or just say, "Brexit means Brexit"?
The decision.

Christopher Smith (12)
Litcham School, Litcham

I AM WORRIED

I was worried.
I could not read or write.
I was crying
Because I could not understand.

I use a laptop
Other people knew
That I could not read or write

I know the right questions
I know the right answers
But I still cannot read or write

Who can I ask?
My parents? My teachers? My friends?
I ask them and they try

I still cannot read or write
I cry
I am worried
But I do try

I hope they understand
Why, oh *why*?

Stanton Moody (11)
Litcham School, Litcham

I MISS HER

I miss her,
The way she always made me laugh
The way she always made me watch
Another film with her,
When you're so close to someone, like I was to her,
They're always with you, like you're attached
By an invisible string,
You can always feel her with you
Even though you're so far apart.
But now she is gone when I reach for her
I fall into a deep pit of nothing
The only thing that keeps me going
Is the sound of her laugh
I miss her,
And I love her.

Lizzie Daw (12)
Litcham School, Litcham

I GET BULLIED

I get bullied.
It hurts me really bad,
Also makes me distraught
And makes me go mad

The big, bright, bold, bully-
What's going on in your life?
Do you understand me fully?
By putting me through all this strife.

People don't like me,
They treat me like a pea,
Sometimes I feel so small,
Because of how they treat me.

Pardon me,
I'm still here
Stop treating me like
You can't see me.
I can still hear
You...

Abi Foulsham (13)
Litcham School, Litcham

CHANGING CLIMATE

Ice caps melting
Polar bears and penguins dying
Yet people still think
It's not real
These are the people who destroy our society

People can't see
The danger that they are making
With the fumes they create
Yet they still deny
And they don't realise their fate

So I say to people
Don't deny
Stand above the people who do
Don't believe their lies
Stand above this corrupt system

End of transmission.

Dominic Hancock-Boggust (14)
Litcham School, Litcham

WHAT IT BOILS DOWN TO

Some eggs are white and others are brown,
but once you peel off the hard, outer shell,
on the inside, all eggs are the same,
they all have a bleeding heart.

When an egg is thrown into the mix,
the shape and structure changes,
no longer its stable self,
the walls of safety have been broken.

A cracked exterior and a blemished skin,
does not affect the inside,
You must first learn to look past the outer shell,
to find the inner beauty.

Alysha Jolie West (14)
Litcham School, Litcham

MY PRECIOUS BOY

He was a boy,
trapped in his own world,
his thoughts took him away,
as his whole life swirled,
he had a mind,
unlike yours and mine,
and yet he had a smile,
that could make the world shine.
When he goes, I miss him,
because I do love him deeply,
he means the universe and more,
although he is indeed cheeky,
but no matter what happens,
I'll always be there for him,
because this boy is my brother,
and his name is Benjamin.

Chloe Cunnell-Westhorpe (12)
Litcham School, Litcham

DIABETES

Diabetes is bad but not as bad as others
I may be scared but others are too
It's with me for life but I do not care

It's too bad but I may not be bothered
I have my lows, I have my highs
But that doesn't stop me
Sugar is bad but not in small portions

I live with it, differently
I'm not tired, I'm sick of the disease
It chose me and it will be with me forever
I don't live with it, diabetes, it lives with me.

Dominic Pickering (12)
Litcham School, Litcham

THE FEELING OF GETTING LOST IN A BOOK

The feeling of getting lost in a book,
Is taking reality away from your mind as you look,
Till there is only imagination,
Now you're in the books location,
You are then suddenly in a boat,
With a baby one-horned goat,
Suddenly, then, you are a wizard,
In your dining hall, eating a gizzard,
Now you're running in a mansion,
Running from a ghost called Stanton.
Then you glance down at your watch,
To find you have read an awful lot!

Magnus Hussmann (12)
Litcham School, Litcham

TUESDAYS ARE TERRIBLE

T in Tuesday is for terrible Tuesdays, never go the way you plan
U in Tuesday is for unbearable day of horror and terror
E in Tuesday is for an everlasting day which never ends
S in Tuesday is for stupid day, which should have never been invented
D in Tuesday is for a day of which you dread thinking about it on a Monday night
A in Tuesday is for atrocious day of hell
Y in Tuesday is for you never forget Tuesdays.

Joshua Deary (12)
Litcham School, Litcham

EVERYTHING

Everything fun, nice, interesting
And more, in everything you do.
Take time,
And enjoy
Everything.
From first walk to first jog,
To first sprint, make it fun,
Because boring shouldn't be
An adjective, no way!
Every day
Have fun
In everything, no matter what happens
In that day.
Problems don't mean
You can't do anything
Or everything.
There should be no boundaries,
Try to do everything.

Jack Daws (12)
Litcham School, Litcham

RIGHTS

He helped me
She helped me
But they only tried, they only risked their lives
They only believed
They all tried for us.

Equality means more to me
She is different, I am only simple
She can do that, I can only do this
She tried, I failed
But she is not perfect
Because there is no such thing as perfect.

Not trying is not in my vocabulary
Not helping, not believing
I am scared but
Not to try.

Millie Crosser (11)
Litcham School, Litcham

WAR OR PEACE?

War or peace?
The soldiers decide,
As their hopes decrease,
They choose to fight or to flee.

War means death.
They fight for their lives,
Whilst they catch their breath,
They regret choosing fight.

Peace means life.
They lie in silence,
Glad they didn't use a knife,
As they hope for their country.

War or peace?
He chose war,
Now he will be forever missed,
My dear, my son.

Ollie Jack Boucheron (13)
Litcham School, Litcham

ANIMAL CRUELTY

Why are people cruel to animals?
People who test on animals are bullies
People who are cruel to animals are horrible
Rodents and monkeys, ask them how they feel!

Pet owners can be cruel
They neglect and starve their pets
Animals have feelings too!
Some dogs are put in cages or on chains out in the rain
Dogs are loyal and want to please

How would you feel if you were being tested
Instead of animals?

Blake Paul William Gorham (12)
Litcham School, Litcham

SCOOTING

Whether it's an indoor park
Or riding down the street.

I love scooting along
Using just my feet.

Whether it's a tail whip trick
Or just doing a flare.

People watching just can't help
But look and stare.

If you are a pro you can do a flare
Excitement riding through the air.

With my helmet on just in case I fall,
Riding my two wheels
I feel ten feet tall.

Mikey Troy Futter (11)
Litcham School, Litcham

I AM NOT

I am not a boy,
My hair is short, not long,
A pixie cut, not a ponytail,

I am not ugly,
I don't need to cover my face in make-up
I think I am beautiful how I am

I am not skinny
I am an average weight
Still growing up

I am not a nerd
I enjoy reading and writing
Is that such a crime?

I am not a try-hard,
I care about my grades,
And want success for my future.

Sophie Russell (12)
Litcham School, Litcham

MISSING

I miss you so much
but I can still feel your touch
I prayed to you last night
as I held on tight

I look up and cry a teardrop
upon the floor
I start to cry more and more

Another star means another death,
I miss you so much

It's not the same without you,
that's so true,
you should still be here
holding onto me

I miss you so much, you mean a lot to me.

Amber Hayden (13)
Litcham School, Litcham

BLOOD IS RED, BRUISES ARE BLUE

Roses are red, violets are blue,
You matter and you should know that too.
If you're ever bullied, I know it's tough,
Tell someone or it could get rough,
Anyone will do, parents, friends, and your dog too!
As long as you know, you're amazing,
All of the bullies will be gazing.
Keep safe and enjoy your life without being sad.
Roses are red, violets are blue,
You matter, and you know that too.

Katy Brown (12)
Litcham School, Litcham

DANCE

I love my bedroom
Where I can set free
The dancer inside me.

I can hear the music
When I am on the stage
Standing beside my bed.

The cushions on my bed begin to disappear
Into crowds of people who are
Standing and cheering at me.

As I do my last move and take a bow
I can hear them clapping
Then suddenly, I am brought back to reality
As my mum calls me for my tea.

Amy Brown (12)
Litcham School, Litcham

DISCRIMINATION

Do you think you are better
Because our culture is not the same?
Do you think you have a better chance
At standing up to fame?
Do you think you are a better person
Because our colour is not the same?
Do you think because I'm black,
You can give me negative feedback?
We make our own future, in the end we're all the same,
No matter colour, or religion
It's up to us to make a change!

Reuben Barrett (12)
Litcham School, Litcham

MY FATE

My fate, my fate,
that's for me to choose
My fate, my fate,
how could I ever lose?

My fate, my fate,
no one can change me
My fate, my fate,
I can choose who I want to be

My fate, my fate
I only want to be free
My fate, my fate,
just floating like a bee

My fate, my fate,
that's for me to choose
My fate, my fate,
how could I ever lose?

Brenna Syrad (12)
Litcham School, Litcham

HORSES

Horses galloping wildly along the stream
Drinking water and eating the green
Running wildly along the wind
Waiting for someone to catch me
Not knowing what it would be like
Will I be a jumping horse?
Or a racing one?
Eating chaff and fibre all day long
Having a rug over my tum
What would it be like to be them?
Will I be weak or will I be strong?
Will I be skinny or short?
Me.

Harrison Reeve (12)
Litcham School, Litcham

FAVOURITE SINGERS

Favourite singers mean a lot
They make you think and realise
How much they make you scream and shout
And make you sing their songs

Mostly this happens to girls
And some boys too
And the biggest scare to most people
Is when they notice you!

It's not just their singing
That I want to hear
It's how they make me feel inside
Those words or lyrics, most dear.

Frankie Wright (12)
Litcham School, Litcham

AN EMOTIONAL JOURNEY

S adness is like a scary spirit, making everything seem pointless
A nd
D ays are unbearably long.

T alking to a parent
O r a trusted friend

H elps!
A nd then days feel normal again and you appreciate the
P eople that you talked to more
P lus
Y ou feel like you've accomplished something great!

Harriet Bucher (12)
Litcham School, Litcham

DEVASTATION

Devastation when we go to war,
You fight even after a draw,
Sit here nice and proud,
Wondering what will happen now.

Devastation when we fight,
They shoot while we sword fight,
Lie there, quietly dying,
While the other men are still fighting.

Devastation when I fight,
I shout with all my might,
Silly things that I fight about,
I am devastated.

Isabel Buttle (13)
Litcham School, Litcham

ANTI-BULLYING RAP

Why am I sitting down here?
Looking at people in fear,
I am trying to cheer myself up,
but it's hard when others sneer.

Friends,
Their words are a never-ending arrow in my mind
I don't want to look behind.
Slowly, I gaze around,
but they are already homeward bound.

Alone,
I am left wondering... why?
All I want to do is cry, cry, cry.

Brogan Elliott Knights (12)
Litcham School, Litcham

DIFFERENCES

D ifferences are what make us unique
I ndividuality makes us special
F reedom to be who you want
F reedom to think what you want
E ach one of us is made to be different
R ight to have your own opinions and thoughts
E veryone an individual
N ever trying to be like someone else
T he world needs you to be different.

Cerys Ann Millard (12)
Litcham School, Litcham

ANIMAL TESTING

Motionless, senseless, lifeless,
The light from its once-lit eyes, now lay dull.
Passed in time.
Yet another abused soul, killed for human rights
Isolated from life forever.
Just for us to eat its flesh,
Or use its body for horrid things.
Some never notice it ever had been a living creature.
But here it lies:
Motionless, senseless, lifeless.

Keira O'Sullivan (12)
Litcham School, Litcham

HUMANS

We are black,
We are white,
We are dark,
We are light.

We are European,
We are African,
We are American,
We are Asian.

We are Hindu,
We are Jewish,
We are Christian,
We are Buddhists.

We are together,
We all live on Earth,
We all share the same fate,
We are one.

We are human.

Caleb Bower (14)
Litcham School, Litcham

MY BEST FRIEND

Blonde hair that flows like a
Gentle summer breeze,
Eyes glistening like the blues
Of the seas,
She has a voice that makes
Angels weep,
Standing on a stage
She's beautiful as can be
With all of these fine qualities
It's easy to see that she's
My best friend
And always will be!

Ellie Bishop (12)
Litcham School, Litcham

I AM A MOUNTAIN

Just go,
Just flow,
Just be myself,
I am a mountain.

Just form,
Just storm,
Just create myself,
I am a mountain.

Just rock,
Solid rock,
Just be myself,
I am a mountain.

Walk through the rain,
Walk through the pain,
Just be myself,
I am a mountain.

Jake Friend (12)
Litcham School, Litcham

DREAMS TURNED INTO STARS

Shining, beautiful dreams,
Dreams turned into stars,
Infinite, astral, damaging.
Leaving invisible scars.

Dreams of future and past,
Dreams of fear,
Dreams of happiness,
Dreams of cheer.

Stars, celestial beings,
Stars shining bright,
Stars meaning hope,
Stars giving light.

Lucy Russell (14)
Litcham School, Litcham

BIKES

Bikes help you get fit,
So you don't want to quit,
Why do we have bikes?
It's to travel and help your bones,
To get off your phone,
Do keep them clean,
So they look nice and mean,
Keep your tyres grippy,
So you can stay nippy,
So if you don't want to hike,
Get yourself a bike.

Josh Green (12)
Litcham School, Litcham

EBUNNY

E ats everything
B lack as night
U ncontrollable
N ervous
N aughty
Y ucky to clean out

M aniac
Y oung

R eally cuddly
A dorable
B rown eyes
B ushy fur
I mpish
T ubby.

Dylan Vallerine (11)
Litcham School, Litcham

RIDING

The smell of horses
The country air
The sun
The sounds
The amazing feeling of the wind in your hair
The feeling of the cold
Nipping your cheeks
Making you look like
You have sunburn
I could not imagine
anything else
ever.

Isobel Bowler (12)
Litcham School, Litcham

DEPRESSION

Depression
It's the colour of nothingness
It happens when the door slams and the house rattles
It's the sound of a hoarse voice, tired of screaming
The smell of a hospital when you finally take action
Depression.

Natasha Longley (15)
Litcham School, Litcham

PHONES WILL TAKE OVER THE WORLD

Soon, they'll grow arms.
Then legs.
Then eyes.
Then they'll come together.
Then they'll attack us.
They'll do it, I swear.
Then, we'll be the bird in flappy bird,
In iOS13.13.

Leo Andrews (12)
Litcham School, Litcham

BAD AND GOOD

What is bad and what is good?
War is bad, peace is good
Destruction, climate change and guns are bad
People, peace and hope are good
The world has to have both to be free.

Sarah Fife (11)
Litcham School, Litcham

MY HORSE

People say it's just a horse, but to me, it's more,
he's a best friend, a teacher, and most of all, a leader.

My horse has taught me more than any human ever could,
he will always be the strawberry to my jam.

My horse is my soulmate, this horse made me who I am,
I love him for that.
If I'm ever in trouble, he'll always have my back.

He's like a never-ending dream
except the fact my real horse, called Teddy, is real.

Even grey, sulky clouds smile and shine when they see my horse,
he will always be my best buddy.

No matter how sad or angry my day has made me,
he will always be there for me at home.

Waiting on all fours, standing tall and proud
with his Falabella buddy beside him.

If he had a choice of apple or carrot,
he wouldn't be able to decide!

Daisy Ann Reynolds (12)
Pakefield High School, Pakefield

YOUNG WRITERS INFORMATION

We hope you have enjoyed reading this book – and that you will continue to in the coming years.

If you're a young writer who enjoys reading and creative writing, or the parent of an enthusiastic poet or story writer, do visit our website **www.youngwriters.co.uk**. Here you will find free competitions, workshops and games, as well as recommended reads, a poetry glossary and our blog.

If you would like to order further copies of this book, or any of our other titles, then please give us a call or visit **www.youngwriters.co.uk**.

Young Writers
Remus House
Coltsfoot Drive
Peterborough
PE2 9BF
(01733) 890066
info@youngwriters.co.uk

@YoungWritersUK **@YoungWritersCW**